# Mainly Melancholy

*Poems from Before the Cradle to Beyond the Grave*

This edition first published in paperback by
Michael Terence Publishing in 2022
www.mtp.agency



ISBN 9781800944008

# Contents

# 1:

# Before the Cradle

## There's always next year

The tree's blue lights
Pulse like the life
She's yearned for
For years.
Her monthly pain's
More disappointing
Than any unwanted gift.
She sheds a hot tear
As her nephew
Brandishes a cracker.
She gives him a kiss,
Pulls on the silly hat.
There's always
Next year.

## The ape in the cage

The ape in the cage
Stands to show me
His beautiful body.
I take his proffered finger.
He gazes at my wedding ring.
Then his dark, sad eyes
Meet mine and linger;
Telling me of the misery
He daily must endure.
And I have the strangest feeling
We've lived and loved before.

## The Snowdrop

His Nan was
Laid to rest
Beneath the
Wintry earth.
Said little Joe,
'I will not cry,
'Cos Nan won't die;
She'll come back
To be a
Snowdrop
In the Spring.'

## Re-Born

The catatonic
Caterpillar
In his cosy
Cocoon
Lies upside
Down
Beneath the
Moon.
He longs for the
Cool dawn
And for his
Transition from
Creepy-crawlie
Curious chrysalis
Into beautiful
Fluttering butterfly.
He sleeps;
He dreams
He waits to be
Re-born.

## Age-free beauties

His life had been a pleasure
He'd wanted to live forever,
Was frozen in time;
Work centuries later
To begin again.
He'd sought immortality
But his dream died
When he died
When he realised
His face and body were
Old among a billion
Age-free beauties
Who stared and
Took photos with their
Eyes.

## Precious feet

In the bath
Bubbles form
A warm shawl
Around her shoulders.
Her belly's tight
Round as a boulder.
Its skin pink
Its veins blue.
Girl or boy?
She feels its tiny toes.
They kick,
They splash
In their very first bath.
Such precious feet.
Her baby's almost complete.

# 2:

# Relationships

# Regrets & Secrets...

## What if?

What if I'd gone through
With that pregnancy;
Had my longed-for
Daughter?
Because I know she was a girl.
She'd be twenty now.
Would she be pretty?
Funny?
Clever?
These thoughts have
Haunted.
Hounded.
Confounded me
All these years
And, although I've never confided in
you,
Still frequently reduce me to tears.

**Why didn't I?**

Why didn't I say
'I forgive you.
It's my fault too'?
Instead I watched
You sort for your stuff
Kidding myself that
Enough was enough!
Why didn't I kiss your sad face
As you packed your case?
Why didn't I hold you tight?
Why didn't I put up a fight?
Because the moment went.
The moment went
And you, my love,
Are gone.

## Still Missing

We snogged at
School discos
Back in '73.
Still missing
Your kissing.

## If truth be told

How I miss
Your smiley eyes
Your special kiss
Your kindness to
Old Mr Smith.
I thought the world of you.
If truth be told,
Still do.
But something stopped me
Giving you my All.
Stubborn pride came
Before a fall.
We're now a mere memory to recall.
But, off the record,
You're still adored.

## Her Secret

Beneath a painted smile,
Lips quiver.
Between fake lashes,
Tears shiver.
She carries her secret
Another mile.

## Ice-cream kisses

She wishes she'd never
Shared with him
Those tasty
Ice-cream kisses.
She wishes she'd never
Been tempted by
His good looks,
Charms and riches.
She wishes she'd never
Called his sisters
'Bitches.'
She wishes that she'd
Listened to them
When they said
He had got himself
a new Missus.

## Lamenting

She laments the last moments
Anger overcame her
And robbed her of her
Rehearsed reasonableness.
Words come forth in a burst;
Brought out her worst.
She cursed
The wine
She'd swallowed.
Without it,
They'd never have quarreled.

## Masquerade

Our love was
A sham.
A masquerade.
But many years
Later,
I do wish
I'd stayed.

## The True Me

You'll never know me
Not the true me
Who you never see.
Not the me
Who knows just how
To stand up to you.
Not the me
Who knows exactly
What to do.
The me who will
Tell you when
you're wrong.
The me
Who is strong.
You'll never know me.
Not the true me.
That me
You will
Never see.

## Post-Divorce

To think he'd
Ever thought her pretty!
To think she'd
Ever thought him witty!
They recoil from
Each other's bodies;
Turn their heads
To avoid a greeting,
All the while deepening
The void between them.
Their polarity
A negative energy force
As they attend
Their first shared social event
Post divorce.

## A pinch of salt

She recalls her
Mother's words,
'Don't trust him, my dear,
Take what he tells you
With a pinch of salt.'
Her daughter
Ignored her,
And now adds salt to her bath
To heal and to lick her
Salt-rubbed wounds.
Beneath the sounds of taps a-running
She cries
And her tears raise the level
Of the salt water.

## Alone On-line

A year ago,
as we food-shopped,
We'd laugh as our fingers
Went for the same item
And lingered;
Electric.
Now I do the shopping
On-line.
Alone.
Stroking my phone.
I wish it was you.
I miss you.

## Tiff by Text

What if we'd never had
That tiff by text?
'Can you pick up
Bread?'
'Thought you'd cut out
Bread?'
'Get no wine then.
You're always off your head.'
Tiff by text grew to
'I no longer want to
Share your bed.'
What if there'd be no
Tiff by text?
Would we still be
together?
Not alone, and
Vexed?

## Older, Wiser, Bolder

Each time he saw her
His heart would surge.
'Ask her out!'
His mates would urge.
But he was crippled
With self-doubt.
She'd laugh at him.
He'd go bright red.
And so another
He did wed.
But now he's
Older, wiser, bolder
How he wishes
He'd chanced it,
Risked it,
Been more brave,
Less pessimistic.

## All I need

You'll never know
How hard I've tried
To stop this fight.
You'll never count the
Tears I've cried.
I so regret that night.
You'll never know
How I love you so.
How long I've striven
To put things right.
All I want is to kiss you
And hold you tight.
Please ...
All I need is to be
Forgiven.

## Missing Melissa

Oh wow!
How he wishes
He'd told her
Her homemade meal
Was delicious
And had added a whisper
'But nowhere as tasty
As you are, Melissa.'
Oh wow!
How he wishes he'd
Covered her all
Over with kisses
And insisted on doing
The dishes.
Because now ...
Oh wow!
How he misses his missus.

# Suspicions & Confessions...

## When did you last call me 'Babe'?

When we first met
We even enjoyed
a supermarket trek.
Reaching to bag
The same thing
At the till,
Our fingers would linger.
We felt such a thrill,
Knowing we'd be
Lovemaking
Later,
Then talking
And laughing til three.
Whatever has happened
To you and to me?
When did you last call me 'Babe'?
Why in your sleep
Do you murmer 'Amy'?

## The Wedding

They chat about
The Wedding
Her Hat
Her Dress
The Menu
The Guests
The Favours
For
The Table
The Cake
And oh!
Where to seat
Aunt Mabel?
Of all this
they've spoken.
The Big Day's
Fast approaching.
'I've made a mistake!'
He cries.
And leaves the
Love of his Life
Heartbroken.

## A subtle difference

Back from your gig
Not smelling of sweat
And cigarettes
But of an
Unfamiliar perfume
And spent semen.
The shirt I'd ironed
Sleeve creases
Still sharp.
And there was a
Subtle difference
In your face
Which I couldn't place,
Because your eyes
Refused to
Look at me.

## The Confession

At our wedding party
You become a stranger.
'What's up?' I ask
'Nothing' you say.
Later, made bold by drink,
You whisper in my ear
'I've a confession to make.'
'Even as the confetti
Was settling on your hair,
I knew I didn't really care.
I've always loved another.'
'Look, she's standing
over there.'

## A different man

They used to laugh
and talk for hours
He often used to
bring her flowers
Now he smells of
A perfume
she's never worn
He's begun to wear jeans
with the legs all torn
And since when
was he an Elvis fan?
Oh My God...
He's a different man!
He's even joined a gym
And that's so not him!

## Lies

He touches her hair, says
'Surely a love like ours
Is rare,
When all we want to do
Is share and care?'
'Surely a love like ours
Is unique?
I always know just
what you're thinking,
You don't even need to speak.'
But to his surprise,
There were tears
In her eyes.
'...I've been meaning to talk to you.
I've been telling you lies...'

## Inevitable

He smells of a scent
She's never worn.
He listens to music
they'd never liked.
He puts the coffee jar
on the right.
He has a vacant look
upon his face.
Puzzle pieces
Begin to fall
into place.
And so she begins
to pack her case.
All he's done is to
lie and deceive.
She's come to
the conclusion that
She has to leave.

# Breaking Up
# and Making Up…

**A piece of Me**

When you left,
You took a piece
Of me with you.
A piece of me that
Loved to dance,
That took a chance,
That craved
Romance.
That acted daft
And liked to laugh.
When you left
You took a piece of
Happiness and energy.
Please can you give
The pieces back to me?
I need to pick them up
And start afresh.

## A Sorry Smile

She wiped her face
Free from
Tears of shame,
At last admitting
She should
Take some of
The blame.
She re-tied her hair
In a ribbon of lace,
Painted a sorry smile
Onto her face.
Sighed...
Snapped shut
Her compact,
Quickened
Her pace.

**Their Song**

They'd not spoken
For ages
Angrily cooking tea,
The radio began to play
Their Song.
She refused to meet his eye.
Snapped off the sound.
A more fitting playlist,
her furious
Rattling of pots and pans
And their stony silence,
As she swore to herself
She would never again
sing along.

**Time for Goodbye?**

Bodies apart
We lie
When did this start?
We sigh
Maybe it's time for
Goodbye?
We cry
Now that
Our eyes
Only meet
In the dark.

## All that glitters

'To have and to hold.'
He slid the ring
Upon her finger,
Kissed the bride.
But something
Died.
The ring became
Tarnished,
Old.
Their hugs and
Kisses grew
Cold
Their vows
Turned to
Rows.
And so divorced,
The ring was
Sold.
All that glitters
Is far from
Gold.

## Her blood and tears

Piece by piece
She retrieved the glass
He'd thrown in anger
Until a splinter
Pierced her finger
Made her cry.
Her blood and tears
Smeared the window
Which she wiped
To see his plane
Become a glinting needle,
Stitching up the
Morning sky.

## Escapism

She smiled to
Escape his
Wrath
She changed the
Channel to
Escape his
Shout
She agreed with him to
Escape his
Sarcasm
She kissed him to
Escape his
Anger
She said she'd missed him to
Escape his
Fist
She opened up to him
Silently
Crying
Desperately
Trying
To escape his
Rape.

## The Raft

You've filled a moat
Around yourself
And I can't swim,
Can't stay afloat
And I've no kit
To build a boat,
And, so a raft
I must create
From charm and wit,
My special kiss,
A warm embrace,
Before it's too late.
A raft I'll send to
Mend the rift.

## Hearts Colliding

They'd locked eyes
Across the Town Hall
Dance floor.
She'd smiled shyly
And their hearts collided.
They courted.
The wed.
And then to everybody's joy,
They had a little girl and boy.
But today she saw him with another,
Knew at once it was his lover,
Recalled their hearts colliding,
Felt her hot tears sliding.

## The Baby's Awake

'What's up with you?'
He hissed.
'The baby's awake,'
She replied.
'Ignore it.
I need to be kissed!'
Heart sinking,
She tried to oblige,
But the crying
Grew louder
From the cot by her side.
'Leave it!
I want to be held!
I insist!'
She reached for
Her baby.
Then came
The fist.

*Love is in the Air...*

## A Proper Person

Intrigued by the
Only girl
Who was not
Hunched over,
Stroking her phone,
Who Sat alone.
Teeth like pearls,
Hair all curls.
She looked around the room
Waiting;
Wanting to talk to
A proper person.
Lively.
Volatile.
Beguiled,
He put his own phone firmly
Back in his pocket
And approached.

## Ancient History

Aged twenty
Hugo's favourite place to be
Was in his local library,
Where he could feed his
Thirst for knowledge
Whilst sneaking glances
At Assistant Emily
Who stamped his books
So prettily
That one day,
With ring,
He knelt before her
On one knee.
The rest is
Ancient History.

## Late Arrivals

Both late arrivals
On the post-divorce
Course
Crept to chairs
At the side of the hall.
He dropped his book.
The trainer came him
Such a look!
He cringed.
Now seated beside him,
She grinned.
They shared a smile
Knowing they'd talk
For a while
At coffee break.
An instant rapport.
This could lead
To much more.

## The Story of Kay and Mae

Each day shy Kay
Watches Mae
Over the road
In the small cafe.
She loves how
She walks with
A sexy sway
As she balances
Each and every tray.
Mae always goes
The extra mile.
Then one morning
She gave Kay a wave
And a smile,
'Come, have a cuppa,
Let's chat for a while.'

# 3:

# Health

## Voices in the Void

In bed thoughts fill my head
Telling me all the things I
Should have done or said.
How I wish I could avoid
Those voices in the void.

## Just Once More ...

Try the door
One.
Two.
Three.
Four.
Going to be late.
Reach the gate.
Can't ignore.
Try the door.
One.
Two.
Three.
Four.
Just once more.
One.
Two.
Three...
Wish I could find the key
To unlock his OCD.

## Sleep Paralysis

Her mind awakes,
Tells her she's uncomfy
The way she's lay.
The pillow blocks her nose and mouth
She needs to move;
To breathe.
But her still-sleeping body won't obey.
She must wake him beside her
But her fingers are locked and
Her voice can't make a sound.
Her body is trapped.

## Tinnitus

I seek relief
from the scream in my ear,
the scream that only I can hear,
But to sit in a quiet place
just makes it worse.
Tinnitus.
The curse.

## Painful Kaleiodoscope

My foot's numb.
There's pressure
On my skull.
And then there's the
Piercing warning light.
Another migraine has begun
And I wish I could
Take flight.
I know today
I'll be imprisoned.
Before my eyes
The prism
Grows.
Glows.
Then
Shatters.
Scatters.
Into shards of
Broken mirror.
Silver.
Blue.
Beautiful.
My painful
Private
Kaleidoscope.

## My Private Hell

Safe at home,
Panic attacks me.
I grasp a stair rail,
My Raft,
For if I move,
I'm going to slide off the edge of the world,
and Die.
Shaky;
Dizzy;
Misery.
Dry mouth and eyes;
Pouring pores.
Chest tight;
Lungs fight,
Filled with excess air
They can't expel.
I yearn to feel well.
I yearn to escape
this private
Hell.

# 4:

# Nature and Nice Things

## Nature's Layers

Freshly bathed by
Raindrops
The verdant grass
A willing
Servant's cushion
For a gold and red
Patchwork mattress
Of fallen leaves that have
Bidden farewell
To their
Family tree.
Snow, a soft and bright
Top blanket
Beneath which the grass
Will wake once more
In Spring,
Become a duvet,
Dotted with
Daisies.

## Midnight Feast

Beneath the full moon
She gently picks
Blackberries
From the
Brambles
Where they
Slumber.
Mixes them with a
Magic mixture.
Flour
Soft butter,
Brown sugar.
Bakes for half an hour.
Succulent berries.
Golden crumble.
Finds a spoon.
Great to eat.
Midnight feast.

## Wish we were there

I so wish we could
Bask
In hot sunshine.
Leave our troubles behind.
Drink cold wine
From the vine.
Eat food
Just divine.
Have a laugh
As we splash
In the cool
Of the pool.
Like so many others,
We could do with
Some well-deserved,
Long overdue,
Perfectly sublime,
Re-charging
Time.

## Making way for the moon

Wrapped,
Ready for bed,
In red
Silken sheets,
the tired sun
Vanishes.
Makes way
For the moon.
Rapt in Quink-ink
Blue,
Her ballgown drips
Diamonds.

**Dots ever-moving**

High in the sky
Invisible lines
Connect birds
As they scatter,
An ever-moving
Ever-changing
Dot-to-dot puzzle.

## Fallen Constellation

In the early hours
The island's lights
Pulse.
Throb.
A living,
Breathing
Thing.
Gold and Silver.
A fallen constellation
Calling to its sibling
Stars above
And their crescent mother.
The moon wreathed in cloud
Weeps her consternation.

## The Contented Cat

My cat
Sits close
To the fire,
Stares at the
Flames
As they dance,
Ever change.
Licking and
Flicking and
Teasing and
Pleasing.
My cat
Lays his head
On the rim of his
Basket.
So content
Loudly purrs
Never stirs
Whilst I feed those
Greedy
Flames
More sticks.

## Beseeching Summer to Stay

In last year's tub,
A sad parody
Of pansies grow.
All the yellow and lilac
Smiling faces
And the greenery that had
Embraced the sun
Are now
Long, pale
Tangles.
Stems.
No flowers,
Just tiny leaves,
Weaving their way
And waving their weeny hands;
Beseeching those
Summer days to stay.

**Decisions, decisions...**

I love to travel,
To fly through a
Warm blue sky
Where I soon will
Unravel my stresses,
Wear summer dresses,
Forget all my twinges
And enjoy guilt-free binges.
No decisions to make,
Just which book to take
To the beach
and to make
Sure the suncream's
Within reach.

## The Plastic Windmill

The breeze
Frees
Fractal
Natural patterned
Sycamore leaves.
They flee their family tree.
High-five
Veined fingers
Wave goodbye.
They fall to the ground
With a soft rustling sound.
Sigh.
Resigned.
Retired they
Wrinkle,
Dry,
Die.
Then
Decompose
To help fertilise
A nearby
Seedling rose.

## Needing Nothing

Nearby,
The pool ripples
Turquoise,
Turns a white gull into
A huge, blue
Magical bird.
Young girls look pretty
In their floral frocks,
With their
Big tattoos and
Trainer shoes...
We sit in the sun
With the old folk,
Reading;
Needing
Nothing;
Drinking beer;
Picking
At peanuts;
Nit-picking...
It's great to get away.

## Reluctant to Walk

Holiday's over.
No more
Fab room with sea view,
And their best Prosecco, too.
At five in the morning,
Another sunny day dawning,
A melancholy sound.
Their cases trundle and rattle;
Trail behind them
On the concrete of the complex,
As they choose not to talk,
Like dogs on a lead,
Reluctant to walk.

## Killing Time

As she waits for her plane,
Rain splashes upon the
Airport window pane.
Killing time,
She dreams of
Sunshine,
Sea,
Oranges,
Wine.
Sublime.

## Autumn

Autumn?
That multi-coloured,
Misty pause
Between the Summer
And Santa Claus...

# 5:

# Addiction

# *Ben's Younger Years...*

## Dates in the Dark

Beautiful baby
Brilliant skater boy
My joy
Sold his skates
Then went back to the
Park
For dates in the
Dark
With Drugs
Good lad to Bad
So sad.

## **Believe me, Ben**

Hair gelled in spikes
Beloved trainers
Pristine white
You'd sing and smile
'Reach for the Stars'.
Punch the sky!
All to live for until
Heroin became
your poison high,
Made you steal and
Made me cry...
Afraid you'll die.
But believe me, Ben
I know you have the potential
To live and to love
your life again.

## Sad to say

All smiled who saw
My son jump through the air.
Woolly beanie hat;
Long hair.
Then, one day,
He wasn't there.
Didn't go to the park
Until after dark
And left his skateboard
at home.
Sad to say,
He'd learnt a new
More dangerous way
to play
And to fly through the sky.
On a chemical high.

## Hands High

Hands
High
He'd danced to
Reach for the Stars,
All to live for.
Now he holds up his
Hands,
His needle-marked
Arms,
And his mum helps
Him to dress.

*Ben aged eighteen...*

## Handcuff-Hunched

Handcuff-hunched
behind glass screen.
'Drugs?
Obscene!'
I know he's lied,
can no longer hide.
'But he's still my
Son!'
I cry, and want
To die.

## Dishonour & Disgrace

'Look at your mum's
Face.
Your greed for drugs
Has brought dishonour and
Disgrace!'
She tries to stop her
Tears,
Wishes she could
Turn back the
Years.

## Such a Joyful Boy

Just eighteen,
My son under
Investigation
For drugs-related
Crimes.
Quietly I cry.
The fault is surely mine.
He was such a joyful boy.
We always had such fun.
'Take him
Down!'
I hate the fear upon
his face
I wish that I could
take his place.

**Dream on...**

Addicted
He stole and lied
Sent down!
she cried,
But at least
Inside
He could
Recover
and hide
From
Drugs.
Dream on...
Inside he
met with
Spice,
And now
we barely
live a life.

*Ben in his twenties...*

## Fears & Tears

I plead
But my son
No longer hears
So I hide inside
My fears
and tears
Try a smile;
and wonder
How I can feel
So incredibly
Full
of Emptiness.

## Ammunition

How I wish you'd
Change,
Become
Clean,
Resist the
Drugs
That hold you
Back
Even though you
Have so much to give,
And that prevent the
Life
I know you'd
Love to
Live.
Drugs attack
Your body and
Your mind
And give those who
Don't understand
Or who are unkind
The ammunition
To call you 'Smackhead';
To wish you Dead.

## Promise?...

'Promise?'
'I promise, Mum,'
you say, and make my day
But next time I ring
You slur and you're vague,
You try too hard to speak
with clarity;
to keep within the lines.
Then I know you've lied
and I know I've failed you
and I know I should have
Tried harder.

## The glass I drink from

I despise your lies;
They're see-through like glass.
'Mum, I could do with a tenner.
I have no food.
I need new shoes.
I owe my mate.
I'm in debt.'
You slur;
Off your head,
Today's habit fed.
I despise your lies
They're see-through
Like the glass
I drink from
to forget.

## Trying

Impossible
to get through to you;
to stop the drugs
that make you
stagger and slur
every day.
But I will keep on trying
to prevent you dying.

## Balancing Act

'Sorry, Mum,'
you say as you sway
on your tiptoes then
back to your heels.
Eyes pinpricks;
Arms folded to hide
the lovebite-like
needless
needle marks
on the insides.
He rocks
To and fro.
How does he balance?
I'll never know.
Forward and back
Like our fight against drugs.
What more can I do
But offer help and hugs?

## Your Habit

'Mum,
Every day I turn
A corner,
Slowly but surely
I'm getting clean ...'
Why did I never say,
'I don't believe you,
Son'?
Instead of
'Great! Well done.'
Now I know
You've turned no
Corner.
We're well and
Truly stuck in
Hell.
Grief and guilt
Gnaw at my heart.
Your habit's tearing me
Apart.

**Come on!**

'Please,
Don't do that in front of me.'
She begs her son,
Her voice and her heart
Breaking.
But he tightens the trainer lace
And slaps the bruises.
'Come on!'
Impatient.
Greedy.
Needy.
Her tears the wrapping from
The syringe,
Spits it from his mouth,
Punctures his skin.

## Tourniquet-tight

He pulls the trainer lace
Tourniquet-tight
With what's still
Left of his teeth.
A sharp sting and the
Syringe slides deep
Beneath
His skin
Then spews
Forth the poison
That makes his heart sing,
Whilst his mother's heart breaks.

## My shock?

His trainer lace
A bangle
Dangles
Until he pulls it
Tourniquet-tight;
Holds a syringe
Between his lips,
Tender as a rose.
Slaps his forearm
'Come on!'
Veins rise,
Accept the thorn
Of his needle.
My shock?
That I'm shocked
No longer.

## Breaking Point

Daily
I pray,
But you break your promise
And pierce your veins,
Your drug to annoint.
And I'm left in pieces
I can no longer
Pick up.
At breaking point.

## A poem for Ben

My worst nightmare:
My slowly recovering
Addict son
Slips back to where
It all began.
Because, although I love
You dearly,
Ben,
I could not live through that
Hell
again.

# 6:

# Growing Older

Reminiscing…

## A Veil of Tears

She knew that man;
Reflected in the mirror,
Seated behind her
At the Diner.
His hair now grey,
His lips defined,
He wined and dined
His lady friend.
She knew that man.
Rolling back the years,
She'd last seen him
On their wedding day
Through a veil of tears.

## Memory Lane

'See'
Nan turns a page,
Me at your age!'
A faded girl;
A curl
Just like mine.
A trip down
Memory Lane.
'Make sure you
Do all you can.'
says Nan,
'I wish I could
Live my life over
Again.'

## Once upon a time

Once upon a time
Seems like
Yesterday
There was a
Little girl
Who grew up,
Became
middle-aged,
And now has her
Grandchildren
Round to play.

## True Strength

Let's arm-wrestle, dad!
Who's the strongest?'
I'm old now
And know that
True strength
Is what pulls us through
And Up and Over
The shifting dunes of our
Dreams.
Notching up each
Disappointment,
Hurt, and knockback
Enables us to
Turn a new page.
And so our strength grows
As we age.

## Make a Wish

'No room for
Ninety candles;
Just the one
To light.
Make a wish
And blow with
All your might...'
Dizzied from the
Blow,
Old Jo and her
Dying candle
Grow,

## Calypso Dream

They'd been going for years
To dance at the club,
Growing old, frail
And dusty at the back
Of the pub.
Part of a crowd;
Proudly ignoring the aches.
They waltz …
Slow.
Slow.
Quick-Quick.
Slow.
Wish they were young;
Could escape for some fun;
Calypso on firm sands,
Beneath beaming sun.

## Happy Ever After

A long, long time ago
I believed in fairy tales,
In the slaying of the foe
And the survival of
A sad, young girl
Who would surely grow
Into
A beautiful lady
And marry adorned in wondrous veils
Her tall, dark, handsome
Prince of Wales...
And live happily ever after.

## Clear as Mud

I still recall,
As clear as day,
Dancing to
'Tiger Feet'.
Surprising,
Really,
Because
Now that I'm old,
Most things are
Clear as
Mud.

## Sad Sketches

Seen through
Her tears,
Sepia photographs
From the years
Before he'd asked
Her to become
His wife,
Have become
Sad sketches
Of her
Former life.

## Sealed with a kiss

I recall that writing,
That Quink-ink blue
On Basildon Bond.
I recall that postmark too.
I unfold the pages,
Read slowly for ages,
Then return the letter
To its envelope,
Sealed with a kiss.
Place my hand upon it,
Make a wish.

## My body weeps

Let's reminisce
Find our old pics!...
'Look at your lovely long hair!'
I try not to care.
Tact stops you
Pointing out my
Slim waist;
My unlined face,
But I know it's noted.
'You look so young!'
You say.
'You mean that
I look so old now!'
I cry, and on my
Menopausal bed,
My eyes and
My entire body
Weep
For the loss of my
Youth.

## Old and Beat

'Do you remember
When we laughed and ran
Through thunder
To dance to
'Tiger Feet'?
I often wonder
What became of you,
Now that I'm
Old and beat ...

## Prestige

Once upon a time
Prestige was a
Burgundy bathroom
With bidet;
Scampi and chips
In a basket
On Saturday night
Followed by
Artic Roll
For sweet.
Now prestige is the
Latest phone;
The perfect home,
Complete with
Coffee machine,
In which everything
is seen
Through a screen...
Know what I mean?

## Tommy Potter

1970.
Class 5C.
Jotter full of
Popstar pics;
Marc B.,
Donny and
Even
Cliff.
But back then
My true heart
Belonged to
Tommy Potter;
Even though he
Turned out to be
A Rotter.

## Gran on Repeat

She'd loved to dance
At family do's;
Nothing to lose,
Fuelled by booze.
Her jeans fitting tight,
She'd bop through the night.
Now she stays on her seat,
Tapping fingers and feet,
Ever so slightly off-beat,
Just like her Gran
On repeat...

## Ten years, one month, two days

From the back of the Bistro
I see you seated with another.
She visits the loo
Leaving me
Unsure what to do.
It's been
Ten years,
One month,
Two days.
I notice your hair, like mine,
Has greys.
You must feel my eyes
Burning into your back
Because you turn
to face my gaze...

## Digression

'How are you?'
She remembers those eyes,
Those kind, serious eyes.
'I'm good, thanks'
she replies,
then says,
'I wonder why people say
'I'm good' nowadays,
rather than 'I'm well'?'
He reaches for her hand.
'You digress,'
he says
with a sad smile.
Tries again,
'How are you?...
Honestly?'

*Growing Older*

*with a Smile...*

## Put my life on Pause

Pause my life today,
Whilst I'm not too fat;
Whilst I'm able to walk,
And willing to play.
Pause my life today
Before my face and lips
Become creased and
Corrugated.
Pause my life today
Whilst my memory's still
(almost) sharp.
Put my life on pause
Whilst my grandsons
Still believe in
Santa Claus.

## **Frumpy, Grumpy Woman**

Who's that
In the
Shop window?
That frumpy,
Grumpy woman,
Who no longer
Wears heels,
Or colours
Her hair;
Who no longer
Wears lippy
And doesn't seem
To care?
Who no longer
Pulls in her belly,
And watches
Too much telly
And drinks
Too much wine?
OMG!
It's me...
She really ought to
Stick to tea.

## Slightly off-time

Given half a chance,
I used to love to dance.
Me and my handbag,
First on the floor.
Electric with
Energy,
Fluid with music,
Last through the door.
Now I sit on the
Sideline
Sipping my wine,
Tapping my bag
Which now
sits on my knee...
Slightly off time.

## Who's come to play?

I need an uplift.
I'm down in the dumps.
Tired; old; cold,
I've got the grumps.
Rat-a-tat-tat!
I wearily sigh,
Plod to the door,
Feel I could cry.
But, who's this
Come to play?
It's my little Mae!
I smile and lift
Her way up high...
Just the uplift
I needed to
Make my day!

## The White Lie

'Do you think I've lost weight?'
I ask, admiring myself
In my nice new vest.
Head to one side,
He considers,
'Mmm, no, not really'
He replies.
I think, and almost say,
'It is permissible to tell your aging wife
An occasional white lie.'
But decide to lay it to rest
To throw back another day.

## Unrecognisable

I used to look like you
When I was young
Without a care.
Long, glossy hair;
Fit and slim;
Sag-free skin;
High shoes;
A pretty skirt;
A tendency
To flirt
(just a little).
Now I look at you
And how I hurt.
Apart from the headphones,
I was your double.
Now I'm old;
unrecognisable.

## To Zest a Lime

At fifty
I signed up to the
Quest to find
A New
Zest for Life:
And failed to find it.
Old now,
I no longer lie
That I'd like to
Travel and Party.
I prefer to create
Lives in my notebook;
To potter and to cook.
To smell,
To taste,
To zest a lime
Beats keeping up
With the Quest
To Find the Zest for Life...
Anytime.

# 7:

# Dementia

## I'm no longer Me

Last year,
a pen; a glove.
Now the name of
A Grandson
I love.
My thoughts
Dissolve.
My mind's full of
Holes.
Precious memories
Flee.
I'm no longer
Me.

## What is my name?

My clothes use to be
over there,
but now it's bare
apart from a picture
which I don't like.
'Your stuff is among this lot,' a lady
says,
'Look for your name label inside.'
What *is* my name?
I can't decide.

## Where are we going?

What a palaver
it was to get
Father
into the back
of the car.
He wouldn't
bend in the
right places.
Like a sullen
toddler,
he permits her
to buckle him in.
'Watch your fingers,
I'm closing the door!'
'*Where* are we going?'
he asks her again.
Immensely ashamed,
she pretends
not to hear.

## Full-Circle

Her final words
were lucid.
'When I was
a baby
I wore slip-on
Shoes;
Sucked on food
that was pappy;
Had little hair;
Wore a nappy ...
Yes, I've come
Full-circle.'
She told her carer,
Who said
'Hmmm?'
and continued
to gaze
at her
Mobile phone.

## The disappearance of smiles

Everyone's masked.
Blind-man's buff?
No, that's *eyes* covered.
Can't see,
Like Gran.
I dribble.
Need what?
A hanky
In my pocket
Knotted in case
I forget.
Forget *what*?
I forgot.
I lift my hanky
To my lips
And realise that
I too am wearing
One of those things
That hide your smile.

## The Stranger

Why had I cried
Yesterday?
Or was it
Today?
I can't say for sure.
Had I lost my way
Again?
Did I go to a shop?
The Co-op?
What did I buy
And why?
Did someone
Pop in
For a cup of tea?
There are two mugs
On the drainer.
Was it a carer?
Or was it that
Stranger?

## The Plastic Chair

Once charismatic;
Charming,
But far from
Smarmy,
Now he's pitied;
Sits all alone
In a home
On a chair made from
Plastic.
His behaviour's
Erratic
As he stares through a
Screen at TV shows
He's never seen ...
He used to love to
Read;
But now can no longer
express his
wish or his need.

## Needle in a Haystack

What am I looking for?
Oh yes!
A needle and cotton.
What do I need to sew?
I try to recall,
But I've lost the thread
Of my thoughts.
Perhaps I was looking for a
Needle in a haystack?
How I wish I could
Mend the holes in
My memory;
Stitch them up with
Cotton.
Now, what was it I was searching for?
I've completely forgotten.

## Holes to slip through

My legs walk
me places;
I know not
Where.
My eyes gaze
on faces;
I know not
Who.
I had thought
my mind always
Everlasting;
Not filled with tangles
and holes
to slip through.

## Please release me

Set me free from this ...
What's the word?
... Confusion.
I can't recall
What I've seen
Or heard.
All is blurred.
Time
Undefined.
Ladies in
Uniform
Try to be kind,
But I know I'm a bind;
Slowing them
Down
When they're already
Behind.
Please
Release
Me,
So that I can
Rest in peace ...

## Lost Dreams

My mind's a mess;
A wilderness
Of lost dreams;
A wall of holes
Between
Frail seams,
Through which my
Memories
Flail
Fail
and finally
Fall …

## Yummy Pud-Pud

It's impossible
to return to
being a baby,
Isn't it?...
After all,
Surely I am old;
I have
A great-grandchild
Aged three.
I think his name's Lee.
Yet, my hair is
Now a baby's
Soft cloud,
My mouth,
All gums,
Tooth-free.
I drink from a
Sucky cup,
Wear a nappy
In my cot.
And I'm spoonfed mush
And told
'Yummy, pud-pud,
Mind now, it's hot.'

**A poem for Dad**

Twilight.
When the kitchen fittings,
made sepia-strange,
appear to sit in silence
on the patio;
and the sycamore tree
overhangs our
plates ready for tea.
Inside out.
Overlapping.
Layers of
Reflections,
Is that what it's
like to be you,
Dad?

# 8:

# Diverse Verse

**Start to write...**

Hold onto that dream
Hold it tourniquet-tight
Stitch up that seam
Lest it take flight.
Half-asleep
Seek your pen
Start to write...

## Tantalising

She unwraps a biscuit
Nibbles and
Teases it
Dips it
In her frothy coffee
She licks her lips
But on her mouth a
Crumb still lingers
He wants to brush it off
With his fingers
Then her pink tongue
Flicks out to play
Licks it away.
She looks across
Surprising
Smiling
Tantalising him.

## Insomniac Anonymous

Insomnia found her
Upon a beach
Beneath the stars
and luminous moon.
A piece of paper
Held in place
By a large shell
Caught her eye
Beside the tide,
Yet strangely dry,
She read the poem,
The verse; a curse.
Over the page
the words were worse;
Far more ominous...
Handwritten and penned
By 'Anonymous'.

## Bamboozled

Tonight's stars
of the cocktail bars
begin to sip their gin
through straws.
Pause...
To caress
their phones
with beautiful claws;
take selfies
in their pretty dresses.
Long lashes.
Long tresses.
Sadly later
the giggle of girls
get sick and woozy
Once again bamboozled
by the lure of the booze.

## Saint George's Day

Saint George's flags
on makeshift poles
Flap and Tangle
and Hang
themselves.
Windows are
Cardboard
Or Cracked.
Curtains fail to
Meet in the middle
Instead they gape
And reveal the
Poor addicts inside
Injecting their drugs
To escape.

**Promises, promises...**

I'm sorry
Christmas Day
Was a flop.
Today
I will not drink a drop.
Come,
Let's kiss
And shake my hand.
I promise you
Boxing Day
Will be just
Grand.

## Silly Question

The office clock
Drags its weary hands
To 5 o'clock on Friday.
She yawns and clicks
To close down her
Computer.
She thinks of the wine
Chilling in the fridge
And of a lie-in
In the morning.
Words appear upon her screen,
'Are you sure you want to log-off?'
Now that is irrefutable!

## Breakthrough

He dived
And her heart dived down
To the floor of the pool.
She held her
Breath.
And could hear
No more
Echoey splashes
Or
Squeals
Or waterfall roar
Nor even the grumpy lifeguard's
Whistle or call
Time stood still.
Until he broke through
The turquoise surface,
Shaking jewels from his har.
'I told you I could swim!'
Then
She released from
Her own lungs,
The Air.

## Unhappy New Year

She hears the
Melancholy
Sloshes
From her
Washer,
The solemn
Swooshes of
The Sunday cars.
Her Unhappy New Year
Has begun again.
The circle
Revolves.
Nothing's
Resolved.
She sheds a tear.

## Scrabble

She refuses to be hurried.
She plays the game beautifully.
She lingers;
Licks her lip-sticked lips,
Slowly taps her tapered nails,
And smiles;
Adds 'exqui' to 'site',
'That's me' she purrs,
'Exquisite ...
And even more exquisite,
I'm on a triple-word score.'

## Finding her Smile

She looks at the clock,
Gets a big shock.
She's hit 'Snooze'
Six times, and
Now she's behind.
No time for a drink.
No time to think.
Grabs her bag and her phone,
Has a good moan,
'It's all work and no play...'
Then finds her smile,
'At least it's Friday!'

## Prosecco-Pretty

After a drink
(or maybe three)
I become Wine-Witty
and
Prosecco-Pretty!
I'm a Dashing
Dubonnet-Dancer!
I'm a Sexy
Sangria-Singer!
No more a shy, boring
Minger!
Drink sets me
Free
I'm ha-ha!
Happy!
I'm loving life
No longer fat
Just Cava-Curvy!

# 9:

# Death

## ICU during Covid 19 pandemic

She took my hands,
Wearing plastic gloves
And a bin-bag gown;
Her transparent
Visor, a halo-crown,
Her eyes so
Tired as she looked down.
Her disposable mask
Softened her
Kind white lies.
'He was peaceful
When he died.'

## Perforated Wrists

She'd fill the bath
With deep, hot water.
She'd write a letter
To her daughter.
Then light a candle.
Then fetch a knife.
Her wrists she'd perforate ......
And then she'd join those dots
To solve,
by ending,
The pain-filled puzzle of her life.

## He’s been gone too long

He’d always said,
‘These days, there’s
No need to be late;
Not without explanation.’
She pictures him
In the fast lane;
Checks her phone again.
Opens the blinds;
The paella’s dried;
The wine’s warmed;
The candle’s burned.
Something’s wrong.
He’s been gone too long.

## Our Song

'Remember our wedding?...'
His hand holds hers
Upon the hospice bedding,
'...Our song?'
*You are my sunshine,*
*My only sunshine,*
*You make me happy*
*When skies are grey...*
'Nurse!'
He cries,
'She's getting worse!'
*You are my sunshine...*
'I'm sorry, my dear,
She's in decline.'
*... Please don't take*
*My sunshine away ...'*

**So Much Unsaid...**

She left him
Just a room
of Stuff;
An unmade bed;
Half a loaf of bread;
A book part-read
So much unsaid.
Bin?
Charity?
Keep?
He begins to
Weep.

## Ever-deepening water

In her bath,
coffin-sized,
she wipes eyes
which are weeping
into water ever-deepening
The ceiling fan hums its
tune from a womb
soon to become a tomb.
Steam and warmth
nd pills and wine
will assist her
deliberate decline.
She submerges
Her face.
Breathes in long.
Submits.
Lies down.
Prepares to
Drown.

## Little Boy Blue

She woke because
the room was silent.
He must have slept through!
Bliss!
Refreshed,
She stretched and yawned,
Gave her still sleeping boyfriend a
kiss;
Drew back the curtains,
Walked to the cot.
Their baby was blue.
A thousand screams.

# 10:

# Beyond the Grave

## Tiny Tears

Time is static
In the attic
Where mum had stored
All our books and toys
For any future
Girls and boys.
I shine a torch
And lift up
My favourite doll;
Forgotten for almost
Sixty years.
She's dressed in just
A fur coat of dust.
I kiss her hair
And then
I swear
I see her tiny tears.

## 'Fur Elise'

I turn the key
To great gran's property,
Go to the living room
Where she no longer
Lives or lingers,
And the doorknob in my hand
Becomes her papery fingers.
A smell of lavender talc,
Then the piano keys move
On their own
All alone,
Playing 'Fur Elise',
Her favourite tune.

**The Lone Virtuoso**

A violinist
She was a lone virtuoso.
Slow Slow
Quick-Quick
Slow.
They waltz to her tune.
They croon
'Fly me to the Moon.'
Tragically, her life
Was taken
Far too soon.
But her music lives on.
That beautiful tone
A virtuoso alone.
Slow Slow
Quick-Quick
Slow.

## A loving message

I pulled
free
the wallpaper
loving
its smell
and how it
curled
and
whirled in
whispering
heaps
round my
feet.
I stretched
up high
to strip a stubborn
square.
Then stopped to
Stare.
A loving message
There
From Daddy
Before he
Died.
I cried a while
And then I smiled.

## Grandpa's Joy

As a boy,
Grandpa's joy
Was his kite.
In the dead
Of night,
I can still
See its flight;
White, billowing
Wing;
Tassel
And String.
And, beneath
The wind,
I can hear Grandpa
Sing.

## Together again

'Don't be morbid!' I'd said,
And you gave me
That special kiss
That I now so miss.
And I'm in bits
As I carry
A pot of bits
Of you
To scatter
In our favourite place;
Where (nearly) all
Our dreams came true ...
But, then, my love
last night I swore
I saw your face,
Then felt your kiss;
Your warm embrace.

**Paranormal Encore**

A haunting melody leaves
Through the window
Upon the frosty October breeze.
It is Beethoven's 'Fur Elise'.
The piano keys
Move all alone
Playing Great Aunt Lorna's
Favourite piece.
I mourn her; I weep ...
We laid her to rest last week!
I applaud her
Paranormal encore.

## The Black Cat's Return

Cautiously,
he opens his door
To a girl in black,
Wearing a
painted,
pointed
cardboard hat.
'Trick or Treat?'
she asks him.
'Treat, please' he says.
Their breath hangs
Between them;
shroud-like in the
Frosty air;
A waiting, vacant
Speech bubble.
A cat appears at
the old man's feet
'Sooty!' he gasps
'But you've been dead for years!'
The little witch smiles;
Then disappears.

## The Plastic Windmill

There is no breeze
In the graveyard.
The leaves on the trees
Are as still and as silent
As the Dead.
And yet, amongst
The wreathes and flowers,
Little Vivienne's
Plastic windmill spins
In loving memory of her
Great Grandad Fred.

*Available worldwide from Amazon*

---

www.mtp.agency

www.facebook.com/mtp.agency

@mtp_agency

Printed in Great Britain
by Amazon